MAR 0 6 2017

P9-CLI-217

United States Regions

Gulf Coast Region

Anastasia Suen

Educational Media

rourkeeducationalmedia.com

Scan for Related Titles
and Teacher Resources

Before Reading:

Building Academic Vocabulary and Background Knowledge

Before reading a book, it is important to tap into what your child or students already know about the topic. This will help them develop their vocabulary, increase their reading comprehension, and make connections across the curriculum.

1. *Look at the cover of the book. What will this book be about?*
2. *What do you already know about the topic?*
3. *Let's study the Table of Contents. What will you learn about in the book's chapters?*
4. *What would you like to learn about this topic? Do you think you might learn about it from this book? Why or why not?*
5. *Use a reading journal to write about your knowledge of this topic. Record what you already know about the topic and what you hope to learn about the topic.*
6. *Read the book.*
7. *In your reading journal, record what you learned about the topic and your response to the book.*
8. *After reading the book complete the activities below.*

Content Area Vocabulary
Read the list. What do these words mean?

barrier
census
culture
hurricane
lagoon
marshes
port
republic
swamps
wetlands

After Reading:

Comprehension and Extension Activity

After reading the book, work on the following questions with your child or students in order to check their level of reading comprehension and content mastery.

1. *How does the tide affect an estuary? (Summarize)*
2. *Which states are located in the Gulf region? (Summarize)*
3. *What did the Louisiana Purchase do for the United States? (Asking questions)*
4. *Why does the government conduct a census? (Infer)*
5. *How can people be prepared for a natural disaster like a hurricane? (Text to self connection)*

Extension Activity

The Gulf Coast region is prone to hurricanes. People who live in this region must be prepared if a hurricane hits. What should they do? Research how to prepare a family and a home for a hurricane. Create a hurricane awareness poster that tells people what to do if a hurricane hits.

Table of Contents

The Gulf Coast Region

The Gulf of Mexico is the ninth largest body of water in the world. Water is always moving. The water that moves here is warm. It flows into the Gulf between Cuba and Mexico. The Gulf Coast region of the United States is made up of the land that borders the Gulf of Mexico. The Gulf Coast states include parts of Florida, Alabama, Mississippi, Louisiana, and Texas.

Much of the Gulf Coast is marshland, where tall grasses and reeds grow in abundance. Birds, fish, and frogs thrive in the **marshes**.

People have lived along the Gulf Coast for thousands of years. Long ago, most people traveled from place to place to find food. We know where they were because we can see what they left behind.

The Karankawa people used arrowheads like these to fish. Artifacts are reminders of long ago people who lived along the Gulf Coast.

Today, many people live along the Gulf Coast region. Many businesses take advantage of the Gulf's resources. Fishing is a big industry for the Gulf. Oil drilling, agriculture, and tourism are also common.

Western Gulf Coast

The western side of the Gulf Coast is in Texas. Many areas of the coast have **barrier** islands. These long, thin islands are just off the coast and are very close to the mainland.

The ocean is on one side of a barrier island. The water on the other side is called a bay.

A barrier island protects the mainland from waves and storms.

Padre Island is a barrier island with salty water on both sides. An area of shallow, salty water near the sea is called a **lagoon**.

South Padre Island, located in Texas, is the southernmost part of the world's longest barrier reef island on the Gulf of Mexico.

The first people to live on the Gulf Coast traveled from place to place. They used bows and arrows to hunt. European explorers came next sailing ships along the coast. The explorers knew that the land at the mouth of the Mississippi River would be very valuable. But it was difficult to rule from Europe. It traded hands several times. Eventually, the United States bought the land from France in the Louisiana Purchase.

Texas has had six flags. First, the Spanish claimed the land. Then France said that Texas was theirs. Later, Texas was part of Mexico. However, it soon declared its independence and became a **republic.** Texas then joined the United States, but succeeded during the Civil War and was temporarily part of the Confederacy.

Did you know that we have a national park in the middle of the Gulf? The Flower Garden Banks is an area of coral reefs.

The Mississippi River

When rivers meet, they flow together. The water from one river flows into the other. All of the water is now going to the same place. Many rivers across the United States flow into the mighty Mississippi River. The Mississippi River flows into the Gulf of Mexico at New Orleans, Louisiana. When most of the country's goods were transported by boat, the Mississippi River was how they traveled.

The Mississippi River begins at Lake Itasca in Minnesota. It ends at the Gulf of Mexico. That's 2,552 miles (4,107 kilometers.)

New Orleans, Louisiana, soon became an important **port** city. People took things down the river to sell them. From the port of New Orleans, goods can be shipped to buyers all over the world.

By 1850, New Orleans was the second busiest port in the United States. It was the fourth largest in the world.

Louisiana has a unique **culture**. When it was controlled by France, French colonists living in Canada moved to the Gulf. This group, known as Cajuns, started a new way of life. Many moved to the **swamps**.

Living with the Creole people already living in the region, Cajun and Creole cultures blended to create unique food, music, and art. Gumbo and jambalaya are two popular dishes from the region.

Zydeco music from the Creoles blended with other cultures and developed into jazz and blues music. Some of the world's best jazz musicians have come from this region.

Louis Armstrong
1901–1971

Fried Catfish

Ingredients:

1 cup yellow cornmeal

1/3 cup all-purpose flour

1 1/4 teaspoons ground red pepper

1/2 teaspoon garlic powder

2 1/2 teaspoons salt

12 catfish fillets

Vegetable oil

Directions:

In a shallow dish, combine cornmeal, flour, red pepper, garlic powder and 2 teaspoons salt. Sprinkle catfish fillets with 1/2 teaspoon salt. Coat each fillet with cornmeal mixture. Cook catfish in 2 tablespoons of hot oil in a nonstick skillet for 5 minutes on each side.

Some catfish live in the salty waters of the Gulf.

16

Many Gulf Coast communities celebrate Mardi Gras, but the elaborate parades and parties of New Orleans are hard to beat. Mardi Gras is celebrated before the Christian Lent begins. People eat traditional food, such as king cake. They watch parades where brass bands play festive music and people wear elaborate costumes.

Southern Coastal Plains

East of the river, the plains begin. At one time, all of this land belonged to Spain. It was called West Florida and East Florida.

With warm temperatures and lots of rainfall, the area was good for plant life. The land was originally covered with thick pine forests. However, much of the forests were harvested for wood. Today, land may be used for farm land. The climate is perfect for growing oranges.

Species-rich longleaf pine forests once stretched across the South, nearly unbroken, from Virginia to Florida to Texas.

Mangroves live in hot, salty water. You can see their roots above the water. They grow in swamps along the coast.

Mangroves can be found in estuaries. These hardy plants can stay alive when the water changes from salty to fresh and back again.

The weather is warm and humid on the Gulf Coast. It rains 40 to 60 inches (101 to 152 centimeters) a year. Near the water in the Gulf, there are swamps and marshes.

There is another plain in south Florida. Most of it is **wetlands**. During the wet season, Lake Okeechobee overflows, and the water moves south. It travels through the grass.

The Gulf Coast also contains a large number of sandy beaches. Grasses grow in the sand dunes and protect the beaches from erosion. The Gulf Coast beaches are a great place to enjoy the sun, go fishing, enjoy surfing, scuba diving, or the many other water-based sports. If water sports aren't your thing, the Gulf Coast region is a bird watcher's dream.

FLORIDA

The Gulf of Mexico

Lake Okeechobee

Airboat Tour

Florida Manatee

Florida Manatees are an endangered species that roam southeast Florida waters.

The Gulf Coast Today

The Gulf Coast is very hot in the summer. Storms blow across the ocean and gain power as they cross the Gulf's warm ocean waters. When the winds reach 74 miles per hour (119 kilometers per hour), the storm is called a **hurricane**. Hurricane season in the Atlantic Ocean is from June 1 to November 30 each year. Many of these hurricanes will move into the Gulf Coast and cause extreme damage to people, homes, and towns in the region.

Pensacola Beach, Florida

Hurricane
Strength Category Chart

Category 1: 74 - 95 mph

Category 2: 96 - 110 mph

Category 3: 111 - 130 mph

Category 4: 131 - 155 mph

Category 5: over 155 mph

A satellite photograph of
Hurricane Irene in August, 2011

When a hurricane reaches land, its strong winds and heavy rain can create extremely large waves, or storm surges. Trees may fall over and cause additional damage. The rain and waves may cause flooding.

Because of the risk of floods, few Gulf Coast homes have basements. When a storm approaches, people should stock up on food, batteries, and other supplies in case the power goes out. They should listen to weather reports in case there is an evacuation.

The city of New Orleans is below sea level. In 2005, Hurricane Katrina broke the levees and flooded the city.

People come to the Gulf Coast for the warm weather. Some people only live there in the winter due to the extreme heat in the summer months.

Some people drive motor homes to the Gulf Coast every year. Because they leave the snowy weather behind, they are called snowbirds.

The government counts all of the people in the country every ten years. This count is called a **census**. It shows who lives where.

Some people live in urban areas or cities with lots of people. Others live in rural areas and small towns. They may live on farms or ranches. The Gulf Coast has both urban and rural areas. It also has some protected areas where no people live at all!

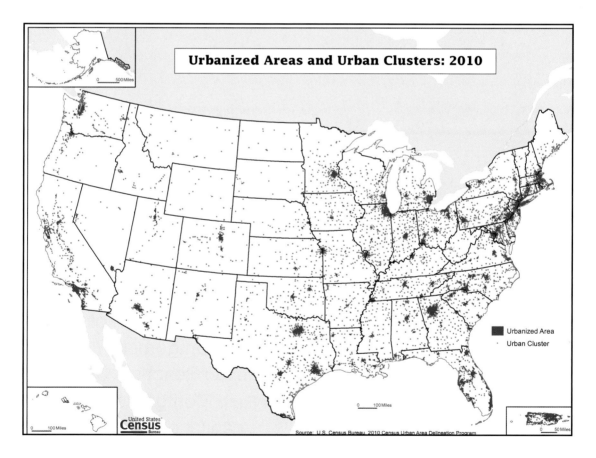

Many people live in urban areas (purple) and urban clusters (green). Few people live in rural (white) areas.

State Facts Sheet

Mississippi

Motto: By Valor and Arms.

Nickname: The Magnolia State

Capital: Jackson

Known for: Mississippi River Boats, Antebellum Mansions

Fun Fact: Root beer was invented in Biloxi in 1898.

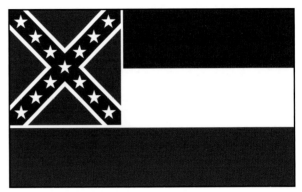

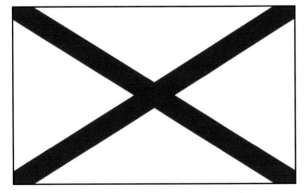

Alabama

Motto: We Dare Maintain our Rights.

Nickname: The Heart of Dixie

Capital: Montgomery

Known for: Beaches, Cotton

Fun Fact: Montgomery was the capital of the Confederate States of America.

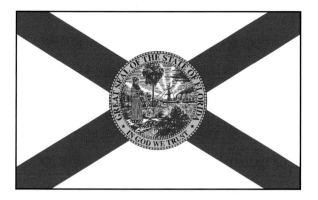

Florida

Motto: In God We Trust.
Nickname: Sunshine State
Capital: Tallahassee
Known for: Beaches, Oranges, Walt Disney World, NASA
Fun Fact: In Spanish, Florida means "Feast of Flowers."

Louisiana

Motto: Union, Justice, and Confidence.
Nickname: The Pelican State
Capital: Baton Rouge
Known for: Jazz Music, Mardi Gras, Cajun Food
Fun Fact: Louisiana is the only state that does not have counties; its land is broken up into parishes.

Texas

Motto: Friendship.
Nickname: The Lone Star State
Capital: Austin
Known for: Longhorn cattle, The Alamo, Cowboys, Oil, Barbecue
Fun Fact: Texas was an independent nation from 1836 to 1845.

Glossary

barrier (BA-ree-ur): something that stops things from going past it

census (SEN-suhss): an official count of all the people in a country

culture (KUHL-chur): ideas, customs, traditions, or way of life of a group of people

hurricane (HUR-uh-kane): a strong storm with high winds that starts in the Atlantic Ocean

lagoon (luh-GOON): a small pool of shallow, salty water near the sea

marshes (MARSH-iz) areas of wet, low land

port (port): a place where boats and ships can dock

republic (ri-PUHB-lik): an independent country with a government of elected representatives

swamps (SWAHMPS): areas of wet, spongy ground

wetlands (WET-landz): land where there is a lot of water in the soil

Index

Show What You Know

1. How do we know that people have lived along the Gulf Coast for thousands of years?
2. What is a barrier island and how does it affect the land and water around it?
3. What kind of plants can grow along the salty, sandy, humid Gulf Coast?
4. Why do so many people come to live along the Gulf Coast every year?
5. What industries are common in the Gulf Coast region?

Websites to Visit

www.nps.gov/pais

www.nps.gov/guis

www.nps.gov/ever

Author

Anastasia Suen lived in Florida as a child and has visited all of the Gulf Coast states. The beach is one of her favorite places. Today she lives in Texas, another Gulf Coast state.

Meet The Author!
www.meetREMauthors.com

© 2015 Rourke Educational Media

www.rourkeeducationalmedia.com

PHOTO CREDITS: Title page © Eric Foltz; page 3 © psasser; page 5 © shaunl; page 6 © mbagdon; page 7 © Linda Bucklin; page 8 © jo11968, negaprion; page 9 © arinahabich; page 10 © Aneese; page 11 © Public Domain, flower garden; page 12 © Wikipedia; page 13 © Antonio Abrignani; page 14 © Toprawman; page 15 © Library of Congress; page 16 © Corid; page 17 © Joel Carillet; page 18 © skiserge1; page 19 © Mazzzur; page 20 © Mark Winfrey; page 21 © Frank Ramspott, daveproth, burdephotography; page 22 © Cheryl Casey; page 23 © Public Domain; page 24 © Jodi jacobson; page 25 © Robert A. Mansker; page 26 © lisafx; page 27 © Public Domain, US Census
Edited by: Jill Sherman

Cover design by: Jen Thomas
Interior design by: Rhea Magaro

Library of Congress PCN Data

Gulf Coast Region / Anastasia Suen
(United States Regions)
ISBN 978-1-62717-672-9 (hard cover)
ISBN 978-1-62717-794-8(soft cover)
ISBN 978-1-62717-911-9 (e-Book)
Library of Congress Control Number: 2014934380

Also Available as:

Printed in the United States of America, North Mankato, Minnesota